T0275294

# Swimming Lessons

# Lili Reinhart

# Swimming Lessons

## Poems

*with illustrations by*

Curt Montgomery

ST. MARTIN'S GRIFFIN
NEW YORK

This is a work of fiction. All of the characters, organizations, and events portrayed in these poems are either products of the author's imagination or are used fictitiously.

First published in the United States by St. Martin's Griffin, an imprint of St. Martin's Publishing Group

SWIMMING LESSONS. Copyright © 2020 by Lili Reinhart. All rights reserved. Printed in the United States of America. For information, address St. Martin's Publishing Group, 120 Broadway, New York, NY 10271.

www.stmartins.com

The Library of Congress Cataloging-in-Publication Data is available upon request.

ISBN 978-1-250-26175-5 (trade paperback)
ISBN 978-1-250-26174-8 (hardcover)
ISBN 978-1-250-26176-2 (ebook)

Our books may be purchased in bulk for promotional, educational, or business use. Please contact your local bookseller or the Macmillan Corporate and Premium Sales Department at 1-800-221-7945, extension 5442, or by email at MacmillanSpecialMarkets@macmillan.com.

First Edition: September 2020

10  9  8  7  6  5  4  3  2  1

To my nana, who always
loved my voice.

# Introduction

I believe that we read poetry to relate to the world.

We see our lives through the words of a poet when we are incapable of expressing ourselves.

I started reading poetry as a way to comfort myself through spells of depression. Discovering poems that closely reflected the thoughts in my own head became re-assuring in a time when I felt severely misunderstood.

It's hard to imagine that anyone out there could possibly feel the same things that you do, to the depths that you feel them. Therein lies the beauty and surprise of poetry.

Once you see that someone understands your feelings, suddenly you're not alone anymore.

I decided a little over a year ago that I wanted to share my own collection of poems in the hopes that they could bring comfort to whomever is looking for it.

The inspiration for this collection came from personal experiences as well as experiences that are not my own. Emotion can be explored and felt through the fabrication of a story, and some of these poems were crafted out of pure empathy for those around me.

Each one of us leads vastly different lives, and yet we can all relate to the fundamental feelings of happiness and sorrow.

I hope that you, the reader, can see yourself reflected in my words.

# Swimming Lessons

I can't seem to write
perfect words
or make them flow as
they should.

They don't sound
particularly profound.

I can't paint you
pretty pictures
or blend colors like
other artists do.

My watercolors don't
bleed beautifully.

But I can say I love you
in as many languages
as you need me to.

I can be fluent in
loving you.

It's been a while since I've had a
moment to miss you,
and to cry.

This warm, summer breeze
on my balcony makes me think of
Cape Cod,
and your floral swimsuits.

How you never wore sunscreen but
always told us we had to.

Even in this loud city,
quiet moments exist where your
spirit is  present.

And I feel like you're sitting next to
me on the beach again.

So I'll wait until the sun goes down
before I go back inside.

For now, we can sit here and listen
to the ocean.

"I love you, darling," were the last words you said to me.

And although I don't have a recording of it,

and although I forgot to save your voicemails,

I will never forget the sound of your voice.

I see you in every flower and every hummingbird
that happens to be near.

I'd like to think that it's your spirit, just saying hello.

You surround me, always.

I miss you.

And I love you, too.

This is how I know
I love you so much.

Whenever I see something
beautiful, I want you to
see it, too.

I seem to be your new
favorite novel.

One that keeps you up
at night,

turning my pages.

Fingers lingering on
me so you don't lose
your place.

you'd think the
sound of this beach
would give me déjà vu,

but it doesn't.

maybe because it's a
different ocean than the one
we used to visit.

maybe because it's November

and I only know the Atlantic
in the summertime.

I hear things a little differently
these days.

the waves sound more
lonely than peaceful.

I'd like to think that
if you were here,
the sun would shine
through the fog
brighter than
it does now.

I find myself missing you
before you're even gone,

Knowing there exists a space
without you next to me.

A *somewhere* I never want to
feel too comfortable in.

My Delilah.

I remember her on our porch,

how she closed her eyes in the sun
as I held her close to me.

I can hear the wind chimes from a
summer afternoon.

I was always clinging to her,
trying to savor our quiet moments.

she knew I loved her, without ever
learning my words

and she loved me right back.

3:24am

The softness of a blink is felt in moments when tears run dry.

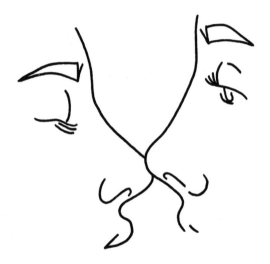

July.

I can still see the
sparkles on the water
and feel the sun on
half of my face.

Sometimes I open my
eyes when we kiss

to see if you're as lost
in me as I am in you.

I want you
in every shade
that you come in.

All the good

and all the bad.

The memories
these walls keep,

I wish they
could speak.

So I could relive
you touching me.

DRUNK

I always want
to make a toast
before we clink
our glasses.

It's my way
of getting to tell you
that I love you.

A profession of my love
disguised by a spirit.

Cheers.

You pointed out the
Big Dipper to me
on the balcony
near the end of summer.

But I'll let myself forget
so you can show me again.

Just tell me more
about the stars,
my love.

Allow me to lose myself
in your constellations.

You let me lay on your clean
sheets and wrap myself in
your damp duvet.

The tumbling washing
machine mixed with the
sound of your video games.

An ordinary day,
an ordinary moment

driving home from work,

with a yellow setting sky
and the windows
cracked open.

I told myself

that I would never let you be
the one that got away.

it seems to be our winter,

so I'll try to make
snow angels in your
cigarette smoke.

he laid down his pen
after a few quiet moments.

and there were no marks
on the corner of the page,
where his hand
had been resting.

the ink had run dry.


there was nothing.


nothing left.

If you give love and project
your heart into the world,

you will receive it in return.

Maybe not right away,

but eventually.

I'm living proof.

I kept loving.
I didn't give up.

And I finally got it back.


Don't give up on what your
heart tells you.

Don't ignore the thoughts
that keep you up at night.

How is it possible

that the moment your
breath meets mine

my lungs become so clear,

it's as if I had been silently
suffocating.

I hope you look at me like
you do the sky.

Standing,

breathless,

admiring my colors.

My heart feels heavy today

but not because of sorrow.

It feels full

or swollen.


It's like I've discovered a new
compartment inside myself

with all this room left to fill.

And I'm filling it,

easily,

with you.

I feel you

latching onto a piece
of myself that will only
continue to grow,

as I grow.


You are engraved in me,

settling comfortably into
my empty spaces.

It's easier for me to talk about *forever*
than it is for you.

You're a present man,

with whom I see this vast,
extraordinary life.


Part of me can't help but dream
about the years to come,

because of this love

that I feel for you now.


I'm anxious to keep loving you

and to create more moments of bliss.


My future is beautiful

because I see the happiness that is
inevitable for me

with you by my side.

I wish I would've kissed you harder
before I left this morning.

how can it be love

if you don't fear
the loss of them.

You have the capacity
to hurt me more than
anyone in this world.

I know

because I've already
felt it.


And this vengeful part
of me wants to hurt you

before you can ever
hurt me again.

I always end up crying
at these local cafés.

What once was beautiful,

is now a somber day.

Driving home with an
empty passenger seat,

an aching reminder of
you leaving me.

You said I had never felt
heartbreak like yours
before.

That once I had,
it would change me.

Only then would I
understand where you
were coming from.

I understand now.

It's just that
neither of us knew
that it would be you.

The heartbreak that
changed me

forever.

When you told me
I had won your heart,

I didn't expect that I
would have to share your
body with anyone else.

You were mine
and yet
you were everyone else's.

I don't need to hear
"I love you" every day

or wake up next to you
every morning.

Just tell me that you
see my face when you
watch the sun rise

and I'll know.

apologies are a
Band-Aid.

the wound is still there,
underneath.

it still hurts,
it just looks cleaner on
the outside.

if I apologized ...
would you be cured?
or is that just a way of
hiding the ugliness
of truth?

the hurt stays.

my "sorry" will never
heal the way you
want it to.

so you might as well
learn to heal yourself ...

without waiting for
anyone else to do it.

And again

the wind is knocked out of me.


My breath is gone.

It reminds me of a dream I had
of you the other night.

Which now I see was a nightmare.

A warning.


That quick, sharp tug that makes
my stomach turn.

And every fucking footstep I hear
outside my door makes my heart
clench and sink.


Because I know it's not you,

coming home to me.

you say that this love
feels different now.

how could it not?

you've broken me.

and I'll never be put
together the same way.

I keep reminding myself that we are
not feeling the same things.
You said so yourself,
I'm more invested than you are.
You're not experiencing this
rejection.

Sitting with one leg crossed over
the other, smoking cigarettes and
turning from me as you exhale,
shifting your attention away.

I'm sitting miles from you, it seems.

Memorizing the curl of smoke
escaping your lips.

Feeling the loss of you,
the strain in my chest when you
forget I'm even here.

And that's what hurts the most.

Feeling this alone.

Mutual heartbreak would be the
only comforting option,
but you can't seem to spare me that.

I let my mind escape

and form these flashes of images
in my head.

Visions of her touching you

and purring at your neck.

The thought of me crossing
your mind for one quick
moment before you shake it off
and indulge.

Practically drooling at the
chance to sabotage yourself.

I am the fighter.
The one who keeps going
and never takes
the easy way out.

In time,
someone eventually
gives way
to collapse.

Just know
it will never
be me.

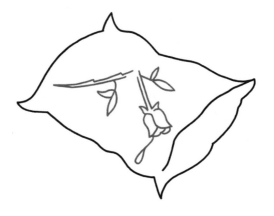

And your lonely, sober mind
will always come back to me.

When the pillow next to you
is vacant

and you've exhausted all of
your distractions.

But keep running.

Brush me off.

I dare you.

That way

in time,

when you see I was right,

you'll feel a sting
on your shoulder

where I once was.

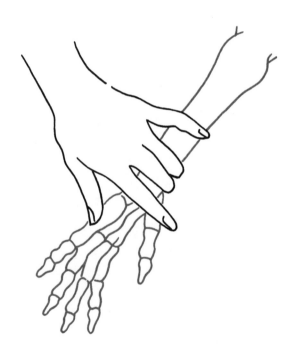

In the beginning

I always felt like
my loving you was

an inconvenience
to your world.

But maybe

the only real inconvenience

was me forcing your hand

into feeling something

that you weren't ready for.

I think you might be
the death of me.

And it's as if I'm running
at full speed
towards my grave.

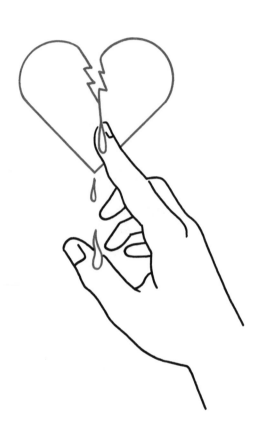

A wound that isn't
cared for festers.

It deepens.

Spreads.

Like a virus under the skin

eventually reaching the brain

and suffocating it.

Heartbreak is a sickness.

A cancer
already in our bodies,
waiting to take over.

Sometimes it's an
inconvenience that can be
patched over.

Our bodies have the ability to
adapt and live on.

Sometimes it's as if we are walking
around with a broken bone

refusing to let it be
put back in place.

And we can
withstand the pain.


To secure protection,

the heart forms a barricade.


A double-edged sword,

often puncturing itself

more than the enemies it's
supposed to keep out.


Puncturing me.

This deep and droning pulse
to love him wasn't a choice.

It was a need

that led me to pursue
this beautiful

but broken

person.

This emotionally unavailable
human being

whose heart was so wrapped
up in fear.

Fear of being vulnerable

and exposed.

Fear of feeding the ache that
was already growing.

But I craved passionate,
overwhelming euphoria.

I wanted that kind of love so
desperately

that I was willing to hurt myself in
order to find it.


I wanted to love him

and so I did.

Through the rejection

and the women,

I was there.

Feeling weak.

I kept offering my heart to someone
who didn't want it.

Humiliating myself within the
pages of a journal that I filled with
thoughts of him.


But it was love.

Overflowing.

And that's what kept me coming back.

The faith I had placed in the words
*your heart will never lead you astray.*

So I kept loving

and I let myself fall.


I welcomed the inevitable
heartbreak.

I accepted the reality that I was a
hopeless romantic.


And when I told him I loved him,
it was because I couldn't hold it in
any longer.

There had been
so many moments

lying next to one another

with my head on his chest,


my eyes stinging with tears.


I desperately wanted
to say "I love you,"

but I was scared

that it would push him away.


Until the overwhelming urge
became too heavy to keep in.

That rainy, gray afternoon

I walked unshielded, under the
clouds.

I held his face in my hands

and said those words.


Words that felt as if they were
crafted for that moment.


And it didn't matter if I was
rejected.

It was pure truth,

whether it was reciprocated
or not.


I cried when I first heard him
say those words back to me,

like a confession.


Something that he hadn't quite
accepted yet.

Something he was afraid to say
out loud because then it would

become real

and he could never take it back.

*᷈᷈*

You can't deny your heart.

It won't be ignored

and it will kick you in the ass
until you accept it.

Through all of my tears and
anxieties,

my fear of never receiving his love,

we came together.

And I believe
I was meant to love him.

To give love to someone who so
desperately needed it

and yet pushed it away fervently.

I didn't step back.

I latched on even harder

and broke through
the walls.

And thank god I did.


How lucky I am to love
someone so much

and to know I can give so
much to one person.

A man who deserves
to be told "I love you," as
many times a day as it
crosses my mind.

don't save me from
whatever universe this is
that allows me to be on the
receiving end of your lips.

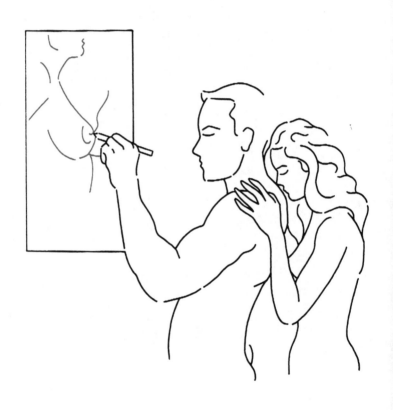

It was wrong of me
to think that this was special

when I wasn't the only one.

I don't know what I thought
would come of this.

I should've known that
everything you said meant
nothing to you

when it meant everything to me.

I never would've gotten involved
had I known you were thinking

and saying

the same words to someone else.

This was a game I didn't agree
to play.

I was never going to compete
for your attention

or love.

And you tried to keep it a secret

as if I wasn't smart enough
to figure it out.

That's the cruel part.

Making me think
I was the one at fault

when you were simply
spinning your wheel
of choice.


I was a fool.

Unknowingly
waiting for you
to choose between me

and other women
with the same
dazed eyes.

the silence
between my questions
and your inability
to answer them
is deafening.

and the pillow
you put between us
before you fall asleep
doesn't go unnoticed.

as if there wasn't
enough of a divide

this should do the trick.

I stopped taking
photos of sunsets
a long time ago.

I can never
capture its colors.

The same goes
for you.

He said "I love you,"
with his eyes closed,

the tip of his nose
resting against mine.

backlit by the sun

with small particles floating
in the air around his head.

our fingers interlaced gently.


I swore I was looking into heaven,

seeing this warm
bright glow behind him.

It was a feeling I don't think
I'll ever experience again,

not entirely the way
I felt it that first time.

But I still feel that warmth,

like a stream of sunlight
being poured into me

moving throughout my body,

when I hear you say those words.

I love you.

Moving away from a crowd

stepping into an empty room

then suddenly forgetting why I
went there in the first place.

Standing still

pausing

wracking my brain for signals

waiting to be told what to do.

On the receiving end of static
radio.

Wandering around slowly

trying to trigger my brain into
remembering the command.

Letting my eyes land on every
piece of fabric in the closet.

Staring at the wispy hairs near
the top of my head in the
bathroom mirror.

Nothing.

No signal coming through.

Waiting

listening

and receiving

static.

This is my looming anxiety
manifested into my morning routine.

A new day should be
a blank slate.

A white room to paint with
endless colors.

But my chest is suddenly tight
and my mind starts to unravel.

Something's wrong

and yet there's no reason behind it.

Why is this happening?

What do I not remember?

This crippling sensation

coming from the center
of my chest

is reaching out for
something to grab onto


and there's nothing.


An uneasy state of being sits there

nestled in close

right as I wake

with no explanation.


So I go back to sleep

and hope that the answer
comes when I wake.

In this aspect, I'll probably
never be like you.

I'll always prefer the familiar
over the unfamiliar.

I prefer the comfort of soft sheets
over stumbling on old cobblestones
through darkly lit streets.

Or maybe I don't.

In truth, I wouldn't know.

I wish I could change

and allow myself to fight
against my own comfort.

Just give me more time.

Keep pulling me
into those moments

and I promise,

one day,

I won't want to go back.

It's been said that
everything you've ever thought
has already been thought before

by someone else.

Everything you've ever said
has been said before

by someone else.

I try to be poetic.

I try to come up with
beautiful words and
make them mean
something,

for you.

Make them sound
as if they haven't
been spoken before.

These poetry books at the
library sit there like
pretentious little fucks

saying "you're too late.
We're already here. We beat you."

Some other sad,

heartbroken,

romantic has managed
to publish their words into the
form of a book

that will likely sit on a shelf

and collect dust for forty years.

But it doesn't matter.

I want my words to collect dust.

Because even if no one reads them,

I'll know that I got there eventually.

Or at least before someone else.

Graffiti.

Another way that humans
can say "I beat you."

Like dogs marking their
territory.

With so much undiscovered
earth and space,

how do we all end up
flocking to the same places?

There are moments where I remember
that I only have this one life.

Maybe you believe in reincarnation

but even if that happens,

you come back
as an entirely different being

in an entirely different life.

You wouldn't even remember the
mistakes you've made as someone else

so how could you learn from them?

A sensation that feels
like the opposite of déjà vu.

It's not that you've been there before,

but that you're only going
to be there once.

You become acutely aware of
how little time you have.

Each day, or month, that passes

can feel like it has little significance.

Until it's five years later

and the realization hits

that you were waiting for a chance to
learn from your mistakes

and you ignored it.

You missed it.

And you absolutely will not get it back,

at least not in this life.

If we could experience those kinds of
moments each day,

where we remember for even one
*second* how little time we have,

would we live differently?


I would drink more.

Indulge in wild, blurred nights.

Stay awake to watch the sun rise

and learn the constellations by heart.

I'd sing loudly

without the consideration of my
neighbors.

I'd fly home on a weekend even if
there were no nonstop flights.

Take beautiful pictures with the
camera I bought, but hardly ever use.

Tell my dad that in elementary school,
I used to say my favorite color
was yellow

because that's what his was ...

and I wanted to be just like him.


I know we wouldn't wait around
as much.

No waiting for signs to point us in the
right direction.

Only following our gut.

I wish I could live this way now.

Because my biggest fear
is waking up in another five years

and realizing that I've wasted so much

of what little time I have left.

the tip of your nose
is cold

and so are your frosty,
pink cheeks.

I put my hands
under your knit hat
and cup your ears,

"these are cold, too."

you smile
and give a little playful grunt
as you shake your head.

you press your nose
against mine

and surprisingly

it's the warmest thing
I've felt all day.

Catching an early flight
and I have to slip away
from your sleepy grip.

You look so small
and innocent,

curled around the
white sheets

in your old man pajamas
that I love.


I kiss your cheek
a few times
and refuel myself
on you.

*Safe travels, baby.*

a single flame
can light up
a room.

that was you, my love.

But it can burn.

also you.

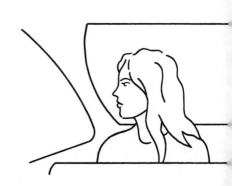

Nothing is
more interesting
than whatever
is outside
the window

when we're alone
in this car.

Silence.

The space
between words
is endless

and your eyes
seem to connect
with everything
except for me.

The seasons hadn't changed in years.

And by the time I put on my first
summer dress

I had forgotten what the sun felt like.

We use people

whether we want to admit it or not.

We use people for moments

or months

or years.

It's a selfish thing we do.

Telling someone
we'll love them forever.

Until that forever ends,
after however long.

You couldn't have fathomed an end
when you were with them,

and now you can't imagine a world
in which you're still there.

Our forevers are so fleeting

they almost mean nothing.

So I stopped saying it.

It's enough to say "I love you,"

and have it end there.

I won't spoil already perfect words
with a time stamp.

Because even forever has an
expiration date.

No always.

No forever.

Just now.

This is how I explain it to someone
who can't fully understand.

I speak with my hands—
they're the most enthusiastic part
of myself.

And I use my body as a map.


*This is me.*

I hold up my right hand,
horizontally, as a vocal
coach does when explaining
the rising pitches of do, re, mi, fa,
and so on.

My hand is at the level of my shoulders.

*This is me.*

*On the day to day.*

*Going through the motions.*
*Mostly steady. Complacent.*
*Low energy.*

*This is you,* I say.

I lift my left hand up,
to my chin.

*This is you, every day.*

*Generally happy.*
*You don't think of each day*
*as "getting by."*
*You're positive.*
*Content.*

*Sometimes we are equal.*
*A good day can make us both*
*feel like this—*

I raise both of my hands to the top of my
head, one on either side of my temple.

*Each hand represents two different people*
*achieving the same state of being.*

*Elated. High. Full of energy. Laughing so*
*hard it hurts your stomach.*

*Of course I am able to feel these things. It's*
*harder to achieve, but I can get there.*

*It's just that I'll have*
*a greater fall back down to reality.*

*To go from here,*
hands at the top of my head,

*to here,*

hands at my shoulders.

*Going from this elation,*
*this joyfulness and ecstasy...*
*to this average, mundane state,*
*can even bring us lower.*

I bring my right hand to my chest.

I refer to this placement
as "rock bottom."

*You can reach the same lows*
*as me, of course,*
*just as I can reach your highs.*

I bring both hands to my chest.

It's no contest.

Certainly not one that anyone can win.

We are just here.

Some of us living slightly above

or slightly below

others.

my head feels claustrophobic
resting in this sink.

my ears are ringing inside this
blue ceramic bowl.

slowly waiting for the water
to sink into my pores
and drown out these flashes
of color behind my eyes.

focus.

for a moment.

then a droning pulse of vibration
every other second.

the faint feeling of spinning
like an optical illusion that
never stops.

parts of my body turning in
opposite directions,

like a merry-go-round

just breathe.

remember to blink.

flex the corners of your mouth.

up.

lift your chin.

not too high.

don't let them see your
empty eyes.

When my hand reaches out
into the empty air,
I like to think that in some
other universe
you're pressing your palm
against mine

and hugging me gently
through the breeze.

I think we're scared to say it.

That maybe you and I just
want different things.

That we are two
fundamentally different
people.

We can't fit into the boxes
that we have drawn for each
other.

And neither one of us

is willing to bend.

I tried explaining to my mother why
I was crying this morning.

It's always different,
the reason or the circumstance.

Today, calling whatever I'm feeling
"depression" doesn't seem to fit.

It's not the right word.

Sometimes it just feels like sadness,
like a dark shadow
mirroring my every move.

I feel numb
yet emotional.

No balance.
No spectrum of white to black.
Just black.

But vast,
so vast that you can lose yourself
in it and forget that you're
staring into a vacuum.

The sun on my face doesn't feel
warm or soft.

It's hot and it burns.

I'm sweating
and itching.

His touch isn't comforting or gentle.
It's unwelcome
and suffocating.

I want to be alone, unbothered.

And then I feel guilty
for being cold,
for not letting in any warmth from
these outside sources.
Innocent volunteers that I'm
shutting down.

It's as if I'm a small, withered person
inside a shell … running on old
fumes and recycling old smiles.
Waiting until my limbs stretch out
and fill my shape again.

Can you just be with me?
Be content.
Lay with me for a long while
without getting bored
or restless.

Find a way to be present in our moments
without a beautiful backdrop,
without a landscape to distract you.

Can you just be with me?

Say "I love you" in a moment that isn't spectacular
just because you want to,
without letting a rare picturesque scene say it for you.

Life doesn't provide a perfect stage.
You will be left longing for moments
that were right in front of you
because you couldn't see how special
something ordinary could be.

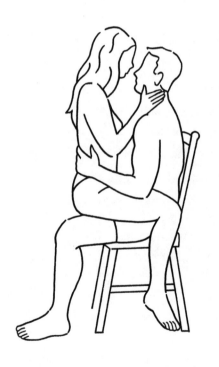

She's beautiful.

And her legs
are wrapped around him
more tightly

than his arms
ever were
around me.

I've had days of loneliness

where I barely spoke

because I had no one
to talk to.

The sound of my own
voice would surprise me,

remind me,

that I wasn't a ghost
floating through the city

going unnoticed.

I was there,

just silently disconnected.

The voice in my head
becoming more familiar
than any of the faces
around me.

We waste so much time
waiting for things to get better.

We pay little attention to the
hours winding down.

The hours we'll want more of
in the end ...

hours that we wish we
hadn't taken for granted.

The idea of complacency
has always terrified me.

I've always been impatient.

In middle school,
I wanted more friends.

I wanted to be better liked
and by more people.

I wanted to be less anxious
and more social.

I wanted to be like
my best friend.
You could pick her face
out of a crowd,
she always seemed to
be shining.

I wanted to move away.
I wanted to be on my own.

Looking back, it seems like
I spent the entirety of my
teenage years in waiting.

There was always something
*more* that I wanted.
And it was always
out of reach.

I felt out of control
in my own life.

My anxiety steered me in
whatever direction it wanted,

regardless of how miserable I was
and how often I prayed
for it to get better.

But it did, eventually

When I took my life
into my own hands
and steered it towards
my future.

Not to say I didn't
crash-land at times,

but that only pushed me
to fight harder

and never settle for anything
less than what I
wanted.

When we throw away our
old bouquets,

we don't regret buying them
in the first place.

We live knowing that there
will be an expiration date.

We don't let it stop us from
accepting the beauty that
lives in small doses.

Nothing is ever wasted.

The beauty of something
doesn't cease to exist just
because it ends.

I was trying to sleep.

I could see the sun
through my closed eyes,
falling on the pillow next to me.

The city's voice outside

mixed with the white noise
of my bedroom.

The stillness of everything.

I remembered an
unremarkable moment

of similar stillness
from a younger time.

The sound outside aligned me with
a former version of myself.

And I suddenly felt the gravity
of my being.

There was a realization of
how much we take in

or rather,

how little of our lives
we actually remember …

and how many small moments
we lose over time.

We're here, every minute,
every hour.

 Yet we only remember
fractions of our lives.

I don't know why this particular
feeling made my heart heavy.

But I found comfort in knowing that
I can find this connection
with myself,

a reminder of my own gravity,
even when I'm not looking for it.

I don't know if I believe in meditation.

I think it's kind of bullshit
but maybe that's because
I've never been able to do it.

How can anyone possibly turn off
their mind and just be?

How do you find a quiet moment
inside of yourself?
Let alone in this loud city.

I try to picture my mind
as being empty.
Tumbleweeds.
White walls.
With no swirling emotions
or rapid heartbeat.


But I still see flashes of thoughts,
like lights turning on and off.
Anxieties, that I quickly try
to push away
only to have them reappear
seconds later.

I can't seem to drop
this acute awareness
or get my footing on this
peaceful ground.

Whoever preaches
meditation as a way of
combating this marathon of
ideas must be lying.
Or else their mind is built in
such a radically different way
than mine.

Someone with my mind has
to take pen to paper to get
the thoughts out,
otherwise they're ricocheting
across my brain
with no pattern and no
brakes.

Many of them are
unreasonable,
as anxieties tend to be.

Projecting emotions that
I think I might have.
Terrified of things that
may never come to
fruition.
Worrying myself to death
over possibilities that are
more fictional than real.

Perhaps, someday
I'll find *somewhere* quiet
enough to drown out the
loud noise that
only I can hear.

Or I'll find *someone*
to help me shut off
my mind.
Rock my anxiety to sleep
and tuck it away
safe
and sound.

I don't know why I came
to this place alone.

I can feel myself slowly
getting drunk.

I feel the burn in my stomach
as the alcohol tries to sit nicely.

I don't even drink,

I only started because of you.

I ordered your favorite food.

I don't know why.

Maybe to summon you,
to feel like you were here
with me.

But the uneaten plate
looks pathetic.

Or maybe that's just me.

I'm getting the two confused.

Maybe I'm just sad and drunk

They seem to be one
and the same.

Maybe each bottle
behind the bartender's head
represents some other sad
person in the world trying to
summon someone

or something.

But the plate stays untouched.

Wasted.

Both of us.

4am.

I built a wall around myself

as our conversation spiraled

and my hope faded.

I wrapped myself in a
blanket

like a shield

and felt the concrete blocks
of the freshly paved wall
around me start to harden.

I slept at the edge of the bed,

far away from the stranger at
the other end.

I'm being turned inside out,

forced to scrape the bottom
of the barrel in order to give
you more of me.

But what happens when you
already have everything?

And you still want more.

What shall I do then?

And how long will it take
for me to lose myself?

when did you become this hardened?

using aggression instead of love.

you've always been strong

but this is different.

this is survival.

this is from being torn down into
rubble and building yourself back up,
forming bricks from crushed
fragments.

who made you this fighter?

who took away your loving self?

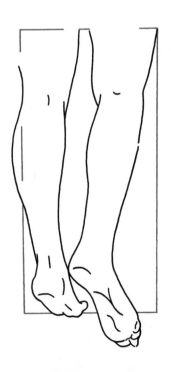

It's sad leaving these
places behind.

It's as if I've buried
pieces of myself here,

tucked away in the sand.

This small moment
is ending,

and I'll never have it back.

I'm lucky enough to have
had it to begin with.

It's a bittersweet ending

when you remember that
time doesn't repeat itself.

There are once in a lifetime
chapters that are finite.

The specificity of these last
few days are only lived once.

That's what makes them
beautiful, I suppose.

The exhilaration in arriving,
knowing new experiences
await you.

Then a somber departure,
knowing those firsts are over.

So here's to making
your mark

and leaving traceable
footsteps behind as you
continue on.

I want to frame that
picture of us,

the one with your hands

wrapped around my waist.

as if we're two dancing
figurines

sculpted into one.

The sound of rain
ceased to exist

and all I felt was the breath
from your lips

like warm summer air
on my neck.

It will always seem
strange to me

to see the flushed faces
of the people who meet
him.

I always notice their
hands trembling,

most too shy to even
look in his eyes.

I can't blame them.

He's beautiful.

Which I call him,

often,

much to his dismay.

"You're so beautiful,"

and he gives me a look
before he smiles in a way
that people do when
they're bad at accepting
compliments.

With millions of
admirers

you'd think it would be
hard to be with only me.

If you could have
anyone in the world,

why would you settle
for one?

But it's not like that.


It is rare to find
someone who sees past
the sea of people who
follow your every move
and hang on your every
word.

I see how rare it is to know
him,

truly know him.

And when he turns from
them
after however long,

he puts his hand into mine.

It's just the two of us again

and I know him better
than anyone in the world.

You are the treasure
I have earned after
multiple lifetimes of
good behavior.

he falls asleep whispering
sweet nothings into my neck.

if his words left their mark,
I'd have no blank space left.

of all the elements,

I'll say that I'm snow.

melting on impact

from your warmth.

I can hear the
piano keys from the
instrumental song
that I love,

when you look at me

with your soft eyes.

The sun came out for us
that day.

After we walked the shoveled path,

elevated above the frozen lake.

My feet sank deep into the snow
and I laughed.

Losing my balance in the
high altitude

with my bare fingers prickling
from the cold.

I didn't feel beautiful that day,

stumbling in front of your lens.

But you capture me in moments that
I've never noticed before.

I see myself through your eyes.

Red cheeks and messy hair that
I'm always moving out of my face.

And the light

from the sun

that came out just for us.

you were a rose
without thorns.

a straight stem with
smooth edges.

poisoned petals were
what you kept from me,

in place of not allowing
my fingers to bleed.

These days I startle so easily
from my sleep.

My body reacts violently
to waking up, as if it was never
intending to do so.

It's like that falling nightmare

falling

falling

waking up with a sharp breath
before I hit the ground

and realize that I'm safe.

But maybe I'm only safe
in my dreams

and the real fall begins
when I wake.

how do you answer your
body's distress call?

how do you drown out the
sound of your own voice?

from a glass, a quarter full,

rolled into thick paper,

or perfectly parallel lines.

how do you self-medicate?

how do you resuscitate
your droning pulse?

standing naked in the
cold air,

lungs hot and screaming.

or with hands up
in some fast car,

blurred red lights
dyeing your skin.

a sense of longing becomes
overwhelmingly present
when I am surrounded by
all of these people.

have I always been
unhappy?

or is it just now?

all of a sudden,

as if I should've seen it
before.

and I'm wondering why I
didn't recognize the long
line of unease.

a string that's been there

all along

underneath

finally becoming untangled.

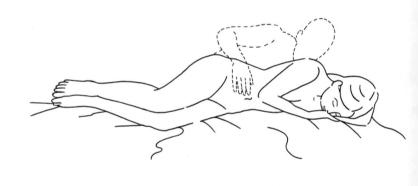

I feel your phantom hand
resting on my waist.

I have to stop myself
from turning around

so as not to confront
your ghost

and the weight of
missing you.

I can feel your breath on
my cheek.

with eyes closed I tilt my
head up towards you

expecting to see your
sleeping face.

but when my eyes open,

the recycled air from
dusty vents

is all that's left to breathe
on me.

for a while I considered you
a misguided step.

until my feet got
comfortable slipping
through the cracks

and I found myself settling
into the grooves of your
worn-out cement.

and I fall,

like a shunned angel
who's been disgraced

back into your folds.

nothing compares to
the hole that I feel

when it hits me
again that I can't
make you happy.

and even my
everything will not
fulfill you.

From the outside

it's hard to imagine why
anyone would stay.

How can she survive
being torn in these different
directions?

She doesn't bend that way.

And yet, she will.

For him.

with our backs
facing towards each other

she could almost pass for you.

I keep thinking that she is.

the tossing under the sheets
sounds the same.

in the dark,

I can't see who's moving anymore—

me or her.

all I know is,

it's not you.
and she never will be.

I never felt
claustrophobic in
crowds until I was
forced into them.

I used to feel like
part of these people
among the masses.

Now I feel like a
rock in the stream

that everything
works its way
around.

I'm still

and unmoving.

Stuck.

While everyone else
is free.

let me be this poem,

this paper lying
unassumingly on your desk.

the napkin for your morning coffee,

to gently graze your lips.

It is a privilege to know you
in such a way that no one else does.

To be the someone who sees
your intimate self so completely.

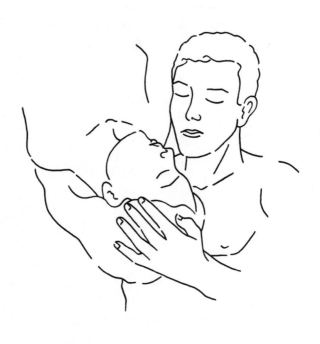

use my chest
to rest your head

I swear I'll never move again.

People wish for me to be this
trailblazing girl.

The one who has marked out a
path for others to follow

on how to be happy,

how to fight when
your limbs feel broken.

Sometimes I feel like a fraud.

But then again,
I never said I was happy.

I've never advertised a cure.

I've only told the world
what I feel,

not how to overcome.

It feels fraudulent to be given
a pat on the back

for simply telling the truth.

Take care of the people
you love

without expecting
a reward

for being a giving and
caring person.

Otherwise you will end
up living in your big,
beautiful house

alone.

Unknowingly homeless.

It's strange to see the world
move on

when someone you love gets
taken from you.

The small space surrounding
you is stuck,

frozen in a moment

of loss

and shock.

Yet the people passing
are continuing on at their
normal pace.

Did they not feel the earth
shake? Or slow?

Can they hear the thoughts
screaming in my head?

Their name.

Their face.

Memories.

Flashes.

Of a friend.

A lost friend.

We always expect the earth
to stand still—

for the universe to grieve
the loved ones we have lost
along with us.

But it keeps moving.

Maybe as a sign that we
should, too.

The movement of strangers,
like a wave, taking us with
them.

So we ebb and flow with the
passage of others,

coasting off their energy
while preserving our own.

Because it's too hard to give
anything right now,

to anyone.

Except for them,

the one we've lost.

And we pray that they're
silently moving in
tandem with us,

guiding us through the
waves when we
can't swim.

Love is the only thing
we can offer one another at this point.

So love really fucking hard.
Always.

# Acknowledgments

First and foremost, I want to thank my beautiful family: Chloe, Tess, Amy, and Dan. I couldn't ask for more supportive parents or encouraging sisters.

Also to my grandparents, Rodney and Corinne, and William and Madeline.

Of course, I couldn't have made this book without the fans who have rallied around me. I am blessed to be on the receiving end of such passionate, encouraging supporters.

To my sweet Delilah, for having been such a source of light in my life.

Thank you to Danie Streisand and Dara Gordon for being the powerhouse duo of agent and manager that you are. Thank you to my entire team: Michael Mahan, Jodi Gottlieb, and Meredith Miller.

Thank you to my team at St. Martin's Publishing Group, and to Sarah Cantin, my editor, who believed in me during the earliest drafts of this book. You took me seriously as a writer and guided me into writing the best possible version of *Swimming Lessons*. I am incredibly grateful for your faith in me.

Thank you to my close friends and loves of my life, you know who you are.